THE CROCODILE AND THE CRANE

Surviving in a Crowded World

THE CROCODILE AND THE CRANE

Surviving in a Crowded World

Judy Cutchins and Ginny Johnston

Foreword by Jonathan Ballou

William Morrow and Company, Inc. • New York

For Lancelot, Butterscotch, and their tamarin family,
Sonya the cheetah, Lady the zebra, and all the
people dedicated to assuring a future for
disappearing species

PHOTO CREDITS
Permission for the following photographs is gratefully acknowledged: Jessie Cohen, pp. 43, 44; Jakki, pp. 39, 40; R. Howard Hunt, Atlanta Zoological Park, p. 10; John Lukas, pp. 2, 21 (top), 26, 27, 29, 35 (top), 50; Wildlife Safari, Winston, Oregon, p. 36. All other photographs by Judy A. Cutchins.

Printed in the United States of America.   1 2 3 4 5 6 7 8 9 10
Library of Congress Cataloging-in-Publication Data
Cutchins, Judy. The crocodile and the crane: surviving in a crowded world. Includes index. Summary: Describes how care and breeding in zoos and other controlled environments have helped protect such endangered species as the wattled crane, Morelet's crocodile, and Arabian oryx. 1. Wildlife conservation—Juvenile literature. 2. Zoo animals—Juvenile literature. [1. Wildlife conservation. 2. Rare animals. 3. Zoo animals] I. Johnston, Ginny.   II. Title. QL83.C88 1986   639.9   86-5339
ISBN 0-688-06304-7   ISBN 0-688-06305-5 (lib. bdg.)

87-15021

Acknowledgments

The authors would like to thank Jonathan Ballou, department of zoological research, National Zoological Park, Washington, D.C.; Dr. Benjamin Beck, primatologist, National Zoological Park; R. Howard Hunt, curator of herpetology, Zoo Atlanta, Atlanta, Georgia; and John Lukas, director, Wildlife Conservation Center, White Oak Plantation, Yulee, Florida, for their expert reading of the manuscript.

We also wish to express sincere thanks to the following people for their assistance during the writing of this book:

James G. Doherty, curator, department of mammalogy, The New York Zoological Society, Bronx, New York; the herpetology staff of Zoo Atlanta, Atlanta, Georgia; John Iaderosa, zoologist, Wildlife Survival Center, St. Catherine's Island, Georgia; James Murtaugh, associate curator in residence, Wildlife Survival Center; Lori Perkins, registrar, Zoo Atlanta; Toni Piccolotti, carnivore keeper, White Oak Plantation, Yulee, Florida; Mike Power, research assistant, National Zoological Park, Washington, D.C.; Alan H. Shoemaker, zoologist, Riverbanks Zoo, Columbia, South Carolina; Kay Taub, department of public affairs, National Zoological Park; Alfred Valenzuela, curator of birds, Wildlife Survival Center.

Foreword

*F*ifty acres a minute. That's how fast rain forests are being cut down. During the same minute, swamps are being drained, grasslands overgrazed and plowed, soil eroded, and water polluted. Valuable animal habitats are being destroyed. It's happening because the world's population is increasing by about 150 people per minute, and people need to have firewood, graze their livestock, and farm the land in order to live.

But the effect on wildlife is devastating. As habitat is decreasing, animals are being hunted, taken as pets, or just simply butchered. Species are going extinct. For many species, there is no hope for survival, yet for others, survival hinges on scientists' and conservationists' efforts to preserve natural habitats, establish captive breeding programs, and eventually release animals back into the wild. For these animals, escape from extinction depends on the temporary refuge of the zoo.

So zoos have been challenged with a task. The challenge is to bring threatened species back from the brink of extinction, hopefully to the point where they can once again be released into a safe natural habitat. This means developing captive breeding programs for crocodiles, monkeys, carnivores, antelope, and birds, to mention only a few. And of course, breeding exotic animals is riddled with complications. No one said it was easy. Each species has its own problems to solve, each may require a unique approach or new insight into the intricacies of zoology and animal behavior. Each is guaranteed to require much work by many different people. So the zoo's challenge is indeed formidable and the consequence of failure grave: the extinction of a unique form of life.

This book describes how zoos are accepting the challenge. It tells of highly motivated and dedicated zoo professionals painstakingly solving captive breeding problems on a species by species case. What do you do when your female cheetah doesn't get along with the male you pair her with? How do you get your endangered crane to lay more eggs? What kind of "survival training" do monkeys need before being released into the jungle? The questions are endless and answering them often takes hours of observing the animal's behavior or even field research of the species in the wild. It may require research into the animal's nutritional requirements or identifying key exhibit requirements to get the animals to breed. Sometimes the answers are as unique as the questions themselves. What works for one species may not work for another, and the zoological detective work begins all over again.

The Arabian oryx and the Morelet's crocodile are just the tip of the iceberg. Captive breeding programs are underway in zoos all over the world for every kind of animal imaginable. Hopefully someday many of these species' populations in zoos will be large and secure enough to begin releasing animals back into natural habitat. But let's hope habitat is still available. As the book concludes, "Captivity for animals is never as good as freedom in the wild." And we've just lost another fifty acres of rainforest.

Jonathan Ballou
Department of Zoological Research
National Zoological Park
Washington, D.C.   1986

Contents

Living in a Crowded World

*T*he earth is home for millions of animal species. Each species is different from the others, yet they have some things in common: all the animals must have food, clean water, fresh air, and a safe place to live and raise their young.

For thousands of years, herds of swift gazelles, handsome zebras, and other species have grazed on tremendous savannas, or grasslands, in Africa. Cheetahs, hyenas, lions, and other predators stalk these grazing herds and kill old, weak, or injured animals for food. The animals share the few precious water holes during long dry seasons.

In the past, tribes of people lived nearby and killed some of the animals for food and for their skins. The populations, or numbers, of both grazing animals and predators changed from year to year, but the grasslands

Zebras once had thousands of miles of grasslands on which to graze.

were so huge that animals of every species survived. The savanna habitat was in balance.

During the last hundred years, the situation has been changing. The natural balance in some parts of the savanna has been upset. The problem is due to the growing number of people in Africa. Humans must have food, water, and space in which to live and raise families. They have plowed and planted some of the grasslands with food crops. People have cut the few scattered trees and burned them as fuel. They have raised large numbers of cattle, sheep, and goats because the savanna makes good pastureland. The herds of livestock stay in one place, overgraze the grasses, and trample the ground.

This leaves dry soil that is easily blown away by the strong winds. Such changes on the savanna make it hard for wildlife to find as much good living space as they need.

The human population of the earth will soon reach five billion! Habitats such as grasslands, jungles, forests, oceans, and even snow-covered mountains are being changed. Surviving in this crowded world is becoming more and more difficult for all wild animal species.

The loss of living space is not the only threat to the world's wildlife. Many rare species are illegally killed, or poached, for their skins, meat, tusks, or horns. The horn of one rhinoceros, for example, is worth thousands of

Rhinoceros horns are valuable to poachers.

dollars. Many people believe they will gain superpower if they use a knife with a rhino-horn handle or take a medicine containing ground-up horn. Even though these superstitions are not true, hundreds of thousands of rhinos have been killed.

For many years, Madagascar's gentle radiated tortoises and the colorful parrots of tropical countries were captured in large numbers because they made interesting pets. Thousands of them were shipped to pet stores around the world. These animals, and hundreds of other kinds, can no longer be legally sold as pets, but the damage has already been done. Their populations are dangerously low.

When the population of a species becomes so small that it may disappear altogether, scientists say it is endangered. If the population drops to zero, the species is extinct. Worldwide, thousands of kinds of plants and animals are near extinction.

In countries where the populations of wild animals are decreasing, conservationists try to convince government officials to set aside large areas of land for the remaining animals. But making laws to protect these natural areas can take many years.

Until they are protected by law, some of the animals are placed in captivity where scientists hope the rare animals will breed, or produce young. To encourage breeding, the scientists provide captive settings that are as

Because many of the large trees used for nesting by the hornbills of Southeast Asia are being cut down for lumber, these colorful birds are almost extinct in the wild.

much like natural habitats as possible. In order to make a captive setting like real life, scientists are spending more time observing wildlife in their remaining wild habitats.

In America and around the world, concerned individuals, corporations, conservation groups, and zoos are spending millions of dollars on captive breeding projects. One of the goals of breeding programs is to raise animals that can be released if land is preserved for them. Another of the goals of captive breeding is to make wild capture unnecessary by sharing animals born in captivity among many zoos. Captive breeding also allows zoologists to study the behavior of animals in captivity. This information, as well as information gathered from studying animals in the wild, is shared with experts around the world to improve captive breeding programs.

It is not possible to rescue all the endangered species. Scientists must choose those species that will adapt well to captive situations. Some species, such as zebras, need large areas. Monkeys, on the other hand, breed well in smaller zoo cages. Some endangered species—the great blue whale, for instance—cannot be raised in captivity at all. This whale needs miles of ocean space and tons of food every day.

Through programs of captive breeding, scientists hope to understand the behavior and needs of these rare animals so they can offer a future in this crowded world for at least some of the disappearing species.

The Crocodile and the Crane tells a few very special stories of the animals in captive breeding programs. Mexico's Morelet's crocodile; the wattled crane, Grévy's zebra, and cheetah of Africa; Brazil's golden lion tamarin; and the Arabian oryx were selected to illustrate wildlife problems in various parts of the world. These animals represent some of the successful captive breeding programs under way in America.

1

Zoo Atlanta Saves the Morelet's Crocodile

A prehistoric-looking Morelet's crocodile lies motionless in the October sunshine. Her large, sharp teeth stick out from powerful jaws, giving the Morelet's a strange smile. Her tiny hatchlings lying close by are just a month old. More than twenty years ago, this mother crocodile, another female, and a two-year-old male were captured in a pond in southeastern Mexico. Scientists knew this species was extremely endangered. The crocodiles were brought to a zoo in Atlanta, Georgia, as part of a special program designed to study and breed the Morelet's. Captive breeding could save the species from extinction.

The Morelet's population in the wild was becoming smaller because, over the years, people had killed large numbers of these crocodiles for their hides. The beautifully patterned skins were made into belts,

Reptiles are valued for their beautifully patterned skins.

Once thought to be extinct, the Morelet's crocodiles
were rediscovered in Mexico in 1923. This male
Morelet's has been part of Zoo Atlanta's captive
breeding project since 1965.

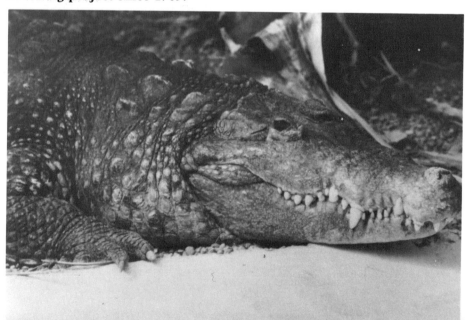

handbags, shoes, wallets, and other expensive leather products.

Another problem for the Morelet's was the loss of their natural habitat. Swamps were drained and filled with dirt to create farmland. Changing the habitat destroyed nesting sites that crocodiles had used for generations.

At Zoo Atlanta, experts tried to copy the crocodile's natural habitat as much as possible. Because they lived in a hot, tropical country, the crocodiles were placed in a special sun-room, or solarium. Today, after twenty years, the Morelet's are still living comfortably in this enclosure. It has glass walls and roof, so sunlight warms the room year round. Along the front of the enclosure, there is a long, deep pool of fresh water. The large room is divided

Banana trees and other tropical plants grow lush and green inside the solarium.

The baby crocodiles are safe under the watchful eye of their huge mother.

into two sections because it is important for adult females to be apart when nesting time comes. Hatchlings and young crocodiles can swim freely from one side to the other, but large crocodiles cannot get through the narrow bars that separate the two sections.

In captivity, the crocodile's natural diet is copied as much as possible, too. Crocodiles are predators that hunt and kill other animals for food. In the solarium, the adults are fed chicken and rats once a week. The younger crocodiles are fed smaller portions of the same diet, and they often catch insects that live in the sunny room.

Resting on a tree branch in the water is a tiny crocodile only ten inches long. He and the other babies hatched from eggs that one of the mother crocodiles had laid that summer.

During the spring before the eggs were laid, zookeepers had observed the male and one of the females mating in the shallow water. A few weeks after mating, the female was expected to build a nest for her eggs. Workers piled wheelbarrow loads of soft dirt and twigs on her side of the solarium. She would use this for nest material.

Day after day, for the whole month of June, zookeepers watched for signs of nest-building. Finally, one morning in early July, she began to work. With her clawed feet, she scraped the loose material into a pile near the banana tree. By the end of the week, her nest was two feet high and four feet wide. Using first one back foot, then the other, the female dug a hole in the center of the nest. It was almost a foot deep when she

During the summer, mother crocodiles dig their nests in mounds of soft soil.

had finished. Crawling over the hole, she laid thirty white eggs, each three inches long. Then, with a back foot, she carefully covered the eggs with soil.

The long wait began. For eighty days, the mother crocodile stayed near the nest. Once in a while, she left to drink from the pool or swim in the cool water, but she quickly returned to the nest. Zoologists continued to observe and make notes on her behavior. Information gathered while studying the Morelet's would be shared with zoologists around the world. Late one evening, one of the zookeepers walked through the dark reptile building with a flashlight. He pointed the light's beam into the solarium. The mother crocodile was still there, standing guard over the nest. Her catlike eyes glowed red in the flashlight's beam.

Hatching time arrived in the early fall. With her front claws, the mother began scratching the dirt on top of the nest. Faint "umph-umph" sounds could be heard beneath the ground. Did she scratch because she heard the babies cry? Or did the babies cry because they could feel their mother scratching up above? Scientists are not sure, but whatever triggered the sounds, the mother crocodile dug quickly into the nest to uncover the hatching babies.

Suddenly, she grasped a hatchling in her powerful jaws and gently carried it to the pool. At the pool's edge, she held the baby between her teeth, allowing water to flow across its tiny body. Then she released the youngster to swim in the shallow water. She returned to the nest and carried the others until all the hatchlings were in the pool. On one trip, she held a dozen babies in her huge mouth. No one is sure why the mother crocodile carries her young when they can walk on their own as soon as they hatch.

For the next month, the young Morelet's crocodiles stayed close to one another. They hung in the water, tails down, with only eyes and snouts showing above the surface. Their tiny legs were outspread to keep them balanced as they floated. Their protective mother was always close by, moving toward them with one stroke of her powerful tail if anything disturbed her babies.

The hatchlings are now a month old and are beginning to explore farther away from one another and from their

Young crocodiles float in the water with only their eyes and snouts above the surface.

Since the crocodile breeding project began, hundreds of Morelet's, like this one, have hatched at the zoo in Atlanta, Georgia. Keepers will remove some of them from the solarium to be raised at other zoos.

mother. The youngsters have been catching insects in the solarium since the day they hatched. They are fed bits of fish and newborn mice, and they have grown rapidly on this diet. Each little Morelet's will grow about one inch a month until it is over six feet long and fully grown.

The breeding program at Zoo Atlanta has been very successful. Since 1970, when the captured females became old enough to lay eggs, they have nested year after year and produced hundreds of young. Zoologists have learned much about the life of this fascinating reptile. Better understanding of this type of crocodile may help to improve captive breeding programs for all crocodile species. Many of the crocodiles raised at Zoo Atlanta have been loaned to zoos around the world. Over a hundred were released in the swamps of Mexico in hopes of increasing the wild population there. But although Morelet's are not known as "man-eaters," people in Mexico do not want to live so close to these large predators, so Mexico wants no more crocodiles released there.

Today there is little space remaining in the wild for these reptiles, and they may soon disappear altogether from Central America and Mexico. But increasing their numbers in captivity can save the Morelet's crocodile from extinction.

Hatching Time at the Wildlife Survival Center

*S*t. Catherine's Island sparkles as the early morning sun beams across the dewy grass. It is April at the Wildlife Survival Center and hatching time for the eggs of the African wattled cranes. Several pairs of this endangered species are living on this small island off the coast of Georgia in an area much like their natural wetland habitat.

Some of the wattled cranes are on loan from zoos across America. The zoos could not provide the large, swampy areas needed by the cranes for successful breeding. So the birds were sent to the Wildlife Survival Center, where the habitat would be better for them. Here, each pair of cranes has a large fenced yard. A small, freshwater stream winds through each pen, making a shallow swamp filled with water plants, insects, frogs, and salamanders for the birds to eat. The

The "wattle" of red, warty skin and white feathers makes this crane species easy to identify.

A wattled crane searches the marshy water for food at the Wildlife Survival Center.

island's temperature is warm almost year round. The wattled cranes have adjusted easily to their new habitat.

One morning earlier in the spring, the center's bird expert and his assistant quietly approached the yard of one wattled crane pair. The men stood outside the fence watching as the female crane probed for food in the wet soil. Her whole body shook as she plunged her beak into the swampy water, searching hungrily for plants.

That morning, the two men had an important job to do, and a difficult one. Wattled cranes normally lay a clutch of only two eggs each spring. The mother crane had just laid her second egg in the nest. The scientists had to take the two eggs from the nest quickly, upsetting the parent cranes as little as possible. Although this seems like a cruel thing to do, it is an important captive breeding method. If the eggs are removed from the nest soon after they are laid, the female will be tricked and will lay two more eggs. This method is called "double-clutching." The number of eggs laid by one female crane is doubled from two to four. The "stolen" eggs are then placed in a heated container called an incubator, where they will hatch. Double-clutching can quickly increase the captive population of an endangered bird species.

The two men stood by the fence waiting for just the right moment to enter the pen. The female waded in the water a good distance from the nest while the father crane stood tall and proud a few feet from the eggs.

Sneaking the eggs away from them would not be easy.

Finally, the men opened the gate and moved slowly toward the large nest. As the two scientists approached, the father crane stretched his long neck and moved closer to the eggs. One of the men waved his arms and ran toward the fence to distract the father. The male crane pumped his wings and followed. Like other captive cranes, he was unable to fly because his wing bones had been trimmed when he was young. The other scientist quickly lifted the two large eggs and placed them gently

The four-foot-wide wattled crane's nest is built of reeds and grasses at the water's edge.

Two wattled crane eggs are carefully carried to the incubator in a bucket filled with soft material.

in a bucket of soft sawdust. Then both men dashed from the pen, avoiding a painful peck from an angry crane.

Just as the scientists hoped, within two weeks the female crane laid another clutch of eggs. This time only one egg was taken to the incubator. The second was left in the nest to be hatched and raised by the parent birds.

The wattled cranes were watched daily as they cared for the remaining egg. Both parents spent time on the nest. The father settled his soft belly feathers over the egg each night, and the mother warmed the egg most of every day.

Now, after thirty-six days, the chick has hatched. Almost immediately, the new baby stands up on tiny, unsteady legs. During the next few weeks, the parent cranes will keep the young chick close to the nest. Taking turns, the adults will probe the shallow water in search of food for themselves and their hungry youngster. Each night, one parent will sleep on the nest with the chick while the other settles down nearby.

Two weeks earlier, the first two wattled crane eggs placed in the incubator hatched. Those chicks are living in a large barn where they are being raised by crane experts. Any day now, the third "stolen" egg will hatch.

In four or five years, these chicks will be old enough to mate and lay eggs. When they grow up, some of these cranes will stay on the Georgia island; others will be sent to zoos as repayment for the breeding loan of their

Soft, downy feathers cover this one-month-old wattled crane chick.

Hidden in the safety of the tall grass, a young crane rests and waits for its parents to return.

Twice each day, the hand-raised chicks are taken for walks to strengthen their tiny leg muscles. In the wild, chicks get exercise by following their parents for a little while each day.

parents. It is hoped that all will have long, healthy lives, choose their own mates, and produce young to increase the population of their species.

Only a few thousand of these southern African birds are living in the wild today, and they are rapidly losing their nesting areas. People are draining the wetlands into nearby streams or rivers to make more farmland and pastures. The cranes and other species cannot survive when their habitat is changed in this way. To conservationists, the cranes have become symbols, representing all the animals and plants threatened by the world's disappearing wetlands.

Some American cranes are endangered species, too. The Florida sandhill cranes have lived in the wetlands of that state for thousands of years. However, the tremendous growth of cities and farms has changed their habitat. Today, there are just three separate flocks left in the wild.

Wattled cranes and sandhills are breeding well in captivity. Members of both species are living at the Wildlife Survival Center on St. Catherine's Island. If some habitats can be saved, they will one day be released into these protected wetlands.

Although Florida sandhill cranes are no longer plentiful in southern wetlands, they are breeding well in captivity.

3

First Steps for
White Oak's Newest Zebra

It is the day after Thanksgiving, rainy but not
very cold. The zoologist in charge of the
zebras huddles under a poncho in the back of a pickup
truck, trying to keep himself and his binoculars dry. He
focuses first on Lady, the eleven-year-old female Grévy's
zebra. The mare is standing quietly on the far side of the
fenced six-acre pasture, apart from the other females. Her
broad, round ears twitch slightly, and her long stiff mane
is standing straight up. Lady is alert and watchful.

Even when she is near the other zebras, Lady is always
easy to identify. The design on each zebra's hindquarters
is unique, like a giant fingerprint. Even the left and right
sides are slightly different.

After checking on Lady, the zoologist shifts his
binoculars to look at the brown-striped foal standing
near her mother in the tall grass. Apparently doing fine,

The black markings on a Grévy's are thinner and closer together than those of any other zebra species.

Lady's one-day-old foal already has a nickname—Baby Girl. She is the newest of the endangered African zebras and the first one ever born at White Oak Plantation, a captive breeding center in Florida. When Baby Girl gets older, her stripes will turn from brown to black, but her individual pattern will never change.

Of the three species of zebra, Grévy's are the largest and most handsome. Unfortunately, poachers have killed many of them for their meat and beautiful skins. The few thousands that remain live in the dry grasslands and rocky hillsides of eastern Africa. Fewer than 250 are in captivity in America, but now there is one more—a healthy new foal at White Oak.

Toward the middle of November, the staff at the

Foals walk on long, wobbly legs when they are just a few hours old.

breeding center had begun looking for signs that Lady and the three other mares were ready to deliver their foals. Several days before Thanksgiving, Lady was seen grazing well away from the other females. From studying Grévy's in the wild, zoologists know a mare usually separates from the herd just before her foal is born. Staff members began a round-the-clock watch for the birth.

From time to time, Lady wandered near the fence line. She moved into the sheltered area and ate some of the grain put out each day for the zebras.

Finally, late on Thanksgiving afternoon, Lady lay down in the tall grass and gave birth to her foal. It was a beautiful, seventy-pound little girl. Lady nuzzled her newborn and brayed softly. Within thirty minutes, the wobbly-legged foal tried to stand. On her third try, Baby Girl kept her balance and took one step before her mother's gentle lick toppled her over. Baby Girl tried to stand a few more times before she and Lady settled down for the night. It was hard to believe, but the scientists knew that this skinny, teetering baby would be running and galloping at full speed before a week had passed.

It has been nearly thirteen months since Lady and the other mares mated with Jack, a majestic ten-year-old stallion. Jack is still at the Florida center, but he is no longer in the same pasture with the mares. Around feeding time, though, his donkeylike grunt and whistle can be heard throughout the pastures. After mating, he had been separated from the mares to make the breeding situation as much like real life as possible. In the wild, female Grévy's often graze together and form temporary herds. Each male, however, stays in his own territory, which may cover as much as four square miles. When the females are ready to mate, they wander into a male's

Females often graze in small herds. Both in captivity and in the wild, they need wide open spaces for grazing.

territory. After a few days, the mares move away, together or separately, toward different grazing places or watering holes, and the male stays behind.

In their African homeland, Grévy's zebras, gazelles, and antelopes graze on the tough, tall grasses, eating only the tender tops of the plants. In many places, the cattle, sheep, and goats have ruined the grasslands by eating the grasses down to the roots and killing the plants. With no roots to hold it, the dusty soil is being blown away. Savannas that used to feed thousands of animals now feed none. These grasslands are no longer in balance, and the animals must move in search of food and water to survive.

Through captive breeding, conservationists are trying to increase the number of Grévy's in captivity. The staff at White Oak will return Jack to the pasture with the mares once all of the foals have been born. Then Lady and the other females will mate with him again. Next winter, perhaps four more foals will be born. If all the foals survive, the size of the herd will be nearly tripled.

The population of Grévy's zebras at White Oak should increase for another reason, too. In captivity, the Grévy's live about twenty-five years, which is much longer than they live in the wild. The grass that they eat in Africa has sand or grit on it. The zebras must chew the tough grass for many hours each day to get enough nourishment to

In captivity, Grévy's graze on tender island grasses. In their African homeland, the grasses are tough and gritty.

stay alive. Because of this constant chewing, a zebra's teeth are worn completely away after about fifteen years, and the animal starves. In Florida, the grass is cleaner and the coastal hay and grain are much easier to chew. With teeth that last longer, the Grévy's survive many more years and so have more opportunity to mate and have young.

The problems for wildlife continue in Africa. For the beautiful zebras, poaching is still a threat. Another problem is the weather. Long periods of time with little or no rainfall dry up the water holes and turn the grasslands into deserts. It is unlikely that captive Grévy's will soon be returned to their African homeland, even if their numbers greatly improve in captivity.

4

Finding a Mate for a Cheetah

Sonya's large golden eyes are instantly alert as she spies the food truck coming toward her pen. Sprinting along the fence line, Sonya shows the grace and speed that make cheetahs the fastest-running animals on earth. As the keeper climbs out of the truck, the sleek, spotted Sonya stretches her long, slender body and purrs loudly. Unlike lions and tigers, cheetahs can purr but they cannot roar. When the keeper opens her gate, Sonya hisses softly and backs away. Raised by people, Sonya is much tamer than most cheetahs. She knows the keeper will not harm her, and she has never tried to bite or scratch.

Each day, the eighty-pound cat gets vitamins and minerals in her three pounds of extra-lean horsemeat. In the wild, Sonya would use her excellent eyesight to stalk a gazelle and her explosive speed to catch it. But she has never hunted her own food. Sonya has been in captivity since her birth six years ago. Today, she lives at the same captive breeding center in Florida as the Grévy's zebras.

The keeper steps back out of the pen after placing Sonya's food near her large wooden shelter. Sitting quietly in the truck, he watches and takes notes on her behavior. Usually, she crouches over her bowl and empties it quickly. But today, Sonya sniffs her food and wanders away. In the far corner of her pen, she rolls over on her back and lifts her feet in the air. This is unusual behavior. It could be a sign that Sonya is ready for a mate. The keeper will watch closely, and if her behavior continues, a male will be introduced to her.

The cubs that Sonya may have will be important to the future of cheetahs. The species is extremely endangered. For centuries, cheetahs lived on the grassy plains of India, southern Asia, and many parts of Africa. Today,

Extra nutrients are added to captive cheetahs' daily diet of ground-up horsemeat.

several thousand remain in the wild, and these live only in Africa.

The cheetah population has become smaller for two reasons. One is because they cannot find enough food. The gazelles and antelopes, which are their favorite prey, have been disappearing from the grasslands. The herds have been driven away by human settlements and livestock. Another reason that the cheetah population is shrinking is that hunters kill them for attacking livestock and for their beautifully spotted fur. The fur of cheetahs and other rare cats cannot legally be brought into America, but not all countries have the same laws as the United States.

For thousands of years, people had captured wild cheetahs. Even though these cats may live as long as fifteen years in captivity, the females seldom had cubs. Wildlife experts worried as the population in zoos, as well as in the wild, steadily decreased.

To protect the cheetahs, laws were passed that prohibited capturing them in the wild and shipping them to zoos. Since 1973, few cheetahs have been brought into America. Many living in zoos are quite old. Unless cubs are raised to take their places when they die, there will someday be no cheetahs in zoos.

Scientists began to study the cheetah more closely. They found that in captivity, females caged with males all the time had very few litters. When zoologists studied

Many cheetahs have been killed for their beautifully spotted fur.

wild cheetahs, they made an important discovery: each female lives alone, unless she is with her cubs. When she is ready to breed, a male comes into her territory. If she accepts him, he stays only a day or two to mate with her.

Zookeepers changed the way they caged their cheetahs and put a male and female together only for breeding. As a result, litters of cubs are born more often. But even with this change, many zoos still do not have success in breeding cheetahs, since females often will not accept the males brought to them. Because White Oak breeding center could provide separate pens for the cheetahs, five females and four males were recently acquired to begin a new captive breeding project.

At the center, keepers observe the females for many hours each day. Although the cats have been at White Oak for over a year, they are still adjusting to their new home. So far only one female, Sonya, has twice shown unusual behavior.

The first time, she paced restlessly around her pen. Keepers introduced her to Chico, a one-hundred-pound male, by moving him to the pen next door to hers. The two cheetahs became acquainted through the fence. After a day, the connecting gate was opened. Chico entered Sonya's pen but did not come close to her. Sonya did not hiss or growl at him. The two completely ignored each other. Sonya did not accept him as her mate. After two weeks, the discouraged keepers led Chico back to his pen.

The next time Sonya became restless, the keepers moved Louie, a two-year-old male, into the pen next to hers. Immediately, Sonya and Louie sniffed and ''talked'' with low purring sounds through the fence. The keepers were hopeful that Sonya would want Louie for a mate. When the connecting gate was opened, Louie bounded in and leaped at Sonya. Swiftly she turned and cuffed him with her paw. The throaty purrs became growls.

In captive breeding centers, males and females are
placed together only for mating.

In captivity, female cheetahs sometimes pace
restlessly around their pens when they are ready to mate.

More litters of cheetahs have been born at Wildlife Safari in Winston, Oregon, than anywhere else in America.

When Sonya walked away, Louie chased her. Sonya hissed as she turned and batted him again. Afraid that Sonya or Louie might get hurt if the two remained together, the keepers returned Louie to his own pen.

Although Sonya and Louie did not mate, zoologists are not going to give up. If Sonya keeps up her unusual behavior, another male will be taken to her pen. Also, one of the other females might accept Chico or Louie for a mate.

If none of the males and females at the center appear interested in one another, the keepers will trade some of them. Locating cheetahs to exchange is not difficult because a special book is kept that lists every cheetah in zoos or captive breeding centers anywhere in the world. Animals are often loaned from one center or zoo to another for breeding purposes. It is hoped that the White Oak project will soon be increasing the population of captive cheetahs.

Because their natural habitat is quickly disappearing in Africa, cheetahs will probably survive only in the largest and best-patrolled nature preserves. With their future in the wild so doubtful, captive breeding programs may be the only hope for the survival of these magnificent cats.

5

Releasing the Little Red Monkey of Brazil

*I*n a small area of tropical rain forest along the coast of Brazil lives the last wild population of one of the world's rarest animals. The tiny golden lion tamarins are very small monkeys, weighing under two pounds apiece. Their beautiful, silky hair hangs like a reddish gold cape over their shoulders. This mane of shiny fur gives them the name "golden lion." The tamarins' clear, intelligent eyes peer out from almost hairless faces. With their lively, impish behavior, it is no wonder golden lion tamarins were once in great demand all over the world as pets and zoo animals. Thousands were trapped and shipped out of the rain forests. By the time it became illegal to capture the little tamarins twenty years ago, only a few hundred were left.

Another serious problem affects the tamarins—the rain forests have been disappearing. Tropical rain forests, or

The squirrel-sized golden lion tamarin is named for its beautiful mane of silky hair. Unlike some monkeys, tamarins cannot hang by their tails. Their long fingers grip the branches as they climb and swing in the forest treetops.

jungles, like those along the coast of Brazil, are home to more species of plants and animals than anywhere else on earth. Yet each day, hundreds of acres are cut for timber and to make more open spaces for farms and cattle. It has been estimated that, worldwide, rain forests are being cut at the unbelievable rate of fifty acres each minute!

For generations, golden lion tamarins have lived in the treetops of the Brazilian rain forests and have fed on fruits, insects, and other small animals. There was always plenty of food, and there were tree holes in which to sleep. But when people needed the land or the lumber, they cut down the trees that supplied food and shelter.

The animals were forced to move into places where they could not survive. Tiny groups of tamarins found scattered patches of forest in which to live, but many could not find mates and start new families. The population became smaller as the habitat disappeared.

Scientists began to study the golden lion tamarins in the wild and in captivity. Zoos were very successful in breeding them. Scientists believed this tiny monkey could be used to meet one of the goals of captive breeding—placing animals in the natural habitat of their species. Conservationists in the United States and Brazil developed a plan to release some of the tamarins from American zoos into the Brazilian rain forest.

Although few tamarins remain in the rain forest, breeding in zoos has increased the captive population.

Just a few years ago, a small preserve near Rio de Janeiro was set aside for wildlife. It was named the Poco das Antas Reserve. Several families of wild golden lion tamarins were already living there. Although the preserve covers only a few square miles, it is safe from saws and bulldozers. In 1984, a few zoo-born tamarins were released into Poco das Antas after being taught to find food on their own.

The release project was successful. Although some of the tamarins did not survive, scientists learned that the younger tamarins and families released together did well.

A second release took place the following year. In the spring of 1985, a family of seven tamarins from the Audubon Zoo in New Orleans, Louisiana, was flown to the National Zoo in Washington, D.C. The family of four-year-old Lancelot, his ten-year-old mate, Butterscotch, and their five youngsters had been selected for the project.

Because the tamarins had been raised in the zoo, they did not know how to live on their own in the wild. Before they could be taken to Brazil for release, they had to be trained for life in the wild. Training would include learning to find food on their own. They were first placed in a room-sized cage at the National Zoo. Vines crisscrossed the cage, and tree trunks with large branches reached to the twelve-foot-high ceiling. Here the tamarins could climb, run, and jump just as they would in the Brazilian rain forest. Lancelot and his family adjusted to the new cage quickly.

During the morning training sessions, the tamarins were fed their normal zoo diet of monkey chow and chopped fruit in a bowl in the middle of the cage. After a few days, zookeepers moved the bowl to a different part of the cage just to change the tamarins' routine a little. Soon more bowls were added and placed all around the cage. After two weeks, the bowls were removed and the food was scattered. Pieces of fruit and chow were hidden under leaves, in hollow logs, or placed on high branches out of sight. Some food was put five feet above the cage floor on top of a post. The hungry tamarins leaped from nearby branches to reach it.

Afternoon sessions were for "prey catch" training. Crickets, mealworms, cockroaches, and baby mice were released inside the cage. The tamarins turned leaves over with their long fingers and searched under bark for their prey. Crickets were the family's favorite, and even the youngest tamarin, nine-month-old Hera, quickly became an expert at catching them. By July, the golden lion tamarin family had learned to search for food just as they would in the rain forest.

After more than two months of training, the tamarins made the long trip by plane to Rio de Janeiro, Brazil. There they spent two more weeks in a large fenced area adjusting to their new rain forest habitat before their

Before captive tamarins are released into the rain forest, they first must be taught to hunt for their own food. This tamarin searches for insects during a training session on "prey catching."

release. Soon the gates were opened, and the tamarins were allowed to explore free of captivity.

Scientists have kept up with the family of Lancelot and Butterscotch since their release. The tiny tamarins appear to be healthy and active. They are gradually exploring their new home, moving greater distances through the forest each day. They search for natural forest foods, but they still return to the release site for food put out by the scientists. Soon they will eat only food they find for themselves.

The golden lion tamarin project is important because it returns a species to its natural habitat. The cooperation and the sharing of information between scientists and governments of different countries will help future release programs.

The best way to help a threatened species is to leave

Scientists provide nest boxes in the rain forest for the newly released tamarin families.

large areas of natural habitat undisturbed. The release of the tamarins into a small preserve is a start in that direction. The endearing charm of the tiny monkeys has won the hearts of Brazilians living around the Poco das Antas Reserve. Scientists hope this love for the tamarins will carry over into concern for the tropical rain forests. Saving the rain forests for the tamarins will also mean saving them for the tree frogs, boa constrictors, butterflies, squirrels, and all the unusual plants that live there.

Educating the people of Brazil about their wildlife takes much work. American and Brazilian conservationists have been reaching the people in many ways. Television and radio programs about conservation are presented regularly. School buses bring groups of children to visit the preserve. But even this is not enough: the teaching must continue.

Zoos are having great success breeding golden lion tamarins, but the outlook for those in the wild is not good. So much of the rain forest has already been destroyed that tamarins do not have much natural habitat left. Only a few families of these monkeys can live in an area as small as Poco das Antas. Whatever the future may hold, scientists and conservationists will not give up on "sauí vermelho," the little red monkey of Brazil.

6

Success in the Desert

One of the greatest success stories of captive breeding is the return of the Arabian oryx to the deserts of Israel. For thousands of years, desert people believed whoever killed an oryx antelope and ate its meat would become strong and brave. The swift-running antelope often escaped from hunters who were on foot or riding on camels. But when trucks and powerful rifles were brought to the desert, the hunters easily killed large numbers of oryxes. By 1960, the beautiful white oryx had become an endangered species.

Conservationists caught a few oryxes and flew them to a zoo in Phoenix, Arizona, for breeding. They called the project Operation Oryx. A few years later, a team of wildlife experts went back to the Arabian desert to capture a few more adults for the breeding program. Not one oryx could be found. The only hope for saving the

A small Arabian oryx herd at the Wildlife Survival Center on St. Catherine's Island, Georgia, is related to those raised in Phoenix for Operation Oryx.

species lay in breeding those few already in captivity.

Fortunately, the oryxes adapted to the Arizona zoo, where the environment was very desertlike. The first calf was born in 1963. Soon there were many more calves, and the size of the herd increased rapidly. The oryxes were divided into small herds and loaned to other zoos and captive breeding centers. By 1979, enough healthy young oryxes had been raised to release a herd into a desert habitat. A group of eleven was flown to the country of Israel and released into one of its nature preserves.

Besides the oryx, many of the spectacular desert animals once native to this habitat had disappeared because of overhunting. Now that preserves had been set aside, the people of Israel wanted to stock them with the variety of wildlife that once lived there. It was fortunate that many of the species were living in zoos and that the zoos were willing to cooperate. Israeli wildlife experts located many of them with the help of a special computer program called ISIS, International Species Inventory System. ISIS was designed to keep track of the location of each member of an endangered species in a zoo or captive breeding center. After an extensive search, the animals of Israel were purchased with government and private money and flown to the preserves in their native land.

Today, gazelles roam the rocky hillsides, and antelopes graze on low brush and grasses just as they did thousands of years ago. Predators such as leopards, hyenas, foxes, eagles, and jackals live in the preserves and feed on the weak, old, or sickly animals. The desert habitat is in balance once again.

The wildlife is protected by guards who patrol the fenced preserves with pride. Hunting, trapping, or poisoning the wildlife is against the law. Thanks to years of conservation education, the people of Israel have learned to share the land with the wildlife. They have a concern for the natural areas and a deep appreciation for the value of nature's balance. The small desert country has set an important example for all the people of the world.

As with the animals of the desert, the survival of the crocodiles, the cranes, and all other species depends on their having a place to live in the future. The population of people, worldwide, increases by 200,000 each day! Their need for food and living space is the biggest threat to wildlife habitats.

Every plant and animal species belongs to one of earth's many habitats. When one species becomes extinct, most of the world does not notice. But each time a species disappears, the natural balance of its habitat is changed a little. Plants and animals that shared its habitat must adapt to the changes or they, too, will die. The system of living things is complex.

More and more, people are beginning to understand that the future of all life, including their own, depends on the preservation of the environment. It is not too late to conserve areas of swamp, desert, forest, and jungle in many countries; but in others, the destruction has already gone too far. As more habitats are destroyed, some animals in zoos and captive breeding centers will be the only ones of their species left in the world. Captivity for animals is never as good as freedom in the wild. Yet captive breeding is one hope for animals fighting to survive in a world that is rapidly taking away their living space. The world's human population will continue to grow. Natural environments must be saved, or there will be no real future for populations of any species.

Healthy babies like this oryx and tiny crane are the best hope for the future of their species.

Glossary

adapt—to fit into, or adjust to, living conditions.

breed—to produce young by hatching or live birth.

captive breeding—to produce young while in captivity.

clutch—nest of eggs.

conservationist—a person concerned about preserving living things and their environments.

double-clutching—removing the eggs from a nest so the mother will lay again.

endangered—threatened with extinction.

environment—the combination of air, food, water, space, and other resources used by a plant or animal.

extinct species—an animal or plant species that has died out completely.

foal—a newborn horse or zebra.

grasslands—grassy plains with patches of scrubby brush and a few trees.

graze—to feed on plants.

habitat—the home of an animal or plant.

incubator—a container that is heated for hatching eggs artificially.

jungle—a tropical rain forest.

litter—all the babies born at the same time to one mother.

livestock—cattle, sheep, goats, and other animals raised by humans.

nature preserve—a protected natural area.

poacher—one who hunts wildlife illegally.

population—a group of individuals of the same species.

predator—an animal that lives by killing and eating other animals.

prey—an animal that is killed and eaten by other animals.

rain forest—a type of forest rich in plant and animal life that is kept green year round by high rainfall and mild temperatures.

savanna—grasslands with grass, shrubs, and a few trees.

species—a group of individuals of the same kind that rarely breed with other kinds.

territory—an area occupied and defended by one species of animal.

wetlands—marshy or swampy areas of shallow water.

zoologist—a scientist specializing in the study of animals and their needs and behaviors.

Index

Photographs are in **boldface.**